Living Today
for God

Living Today for God

(Vivre l'aujourd'hui de Dieu)

by
BROTHER ROGER
Prior of Taizé

The Seabury Press · New York

1981
The Seabury Press
815 Second Avenue
New York, N.Y. 10017

Originally published in France under the title
Vivre l'aujourd'hui de Dieu
Translated by Emily Chisolm and the Brothers
English translation copyright © Les Presses de Taizé 1980

Printed in the United States of America

Library of Congress Catalog Card Number: 81-50004

ISBN: 0-8164-2323-7

This book is intended to stimulate reflection on today's world and today's Church. It was written at Taizé, in a community which tries to take an active part in both the world and the Church, a community acutely aware of the dramatic situation of division among Christians. Perhaps this will endow it with a certain measure of authenticity.

Very many Christians are agreed that our prayer must grow in strength and depth for unity to be achieved. There is much truth in this. Prayer is fundamental, and it is a road open to us all. And yet this prayer necessarily leads us to move ahead in concrete ways. Otherwise it risks being nothing more than a flight from painful realities which would make us refuse to take the next costly step forward.

Today, if you hear his voice, do not harden your hearts . . .   (*Psalm 95*)

Today is the day which the Lord has made; let us be joyful and glad in it.   (*Psalm 118*)

DEDICATED TO
I. ROMERIL

Contents

KEYNOTES OF TODAY'S WORLD

Keynotes of Today's World

Since the fourth century, few periods can have been more decisive than our own. Either modern Christianity will rise to one of the main challenges of the Gospel, the sense of the universal, or else the Christian Churches will turn in upon themselves in those parts of the world where they have taken root, and so obstruct the flow of 'grace, source of salvation for all men'.

Christians are at present confronted with a question of life or death. In the world today there are over a thousand million Christians, divided into a large number of denominations. They look outward towards two or three times as many non-Christians. At the end of this century there will be an estimated six and a half billion people on the earth. And besides the Christians, an atheist ideology is also vigorously striving for unity on a world-wide scale.

If Christians want to show that they are serious about creating communion among all, they must begin by searching for ways of promoting a just distribution of the products of this earth. The countries most densely populated by Christians possess tremendous wealth in comparison with non-Christian countries, devoid of material resources. This is a fact. In the middle of this century, for example, the standard of living in the United States was thirty-five times higher than in India. How this enormous problem is handled may well determine the future of Christianity.

At the same time, are we Christians going to be sufficiently generous, imaginative, and aflame with love, to invent the ways by which we can burst out of the denominational chains at present keeping us captive? And once we have rediscovered a visible communion among Christians, how shall we communicate what we believe to the rest of the world?

What ways can we find of being truly present to the world while still remaining an active part of the Church, the Body of Christ? As we seek to live deeply rooted in the Church, how can we encounter today's humanity and share the best we have to offer: our love of Christ?

Every relationship with Christ leads us towards our neighbours. But a paradox arises, because the established forms of Christianity, as they grow old, tend to separate us from our neighbours, or at least they seem to erect barriers between us and others in our dealings with certain categories of people.

Every return to the Gospel ought to renew our sense of human brotherhood. But our old forms of Christianity are burdened with layer upon layer of civilisation. They seem to trap people and enclose them in a private world of their own.

It far too often happens that members of the official Churches indulge their regressive inclinations and turn towards the past. They are soon left a long way behind what people in general are living today. Often the real motives for such attitudes are not acknowledged. We slip deeper and deeper into the cosy snugness of a Christian society where life is pleasant. Gradually we set up a kind of Christian ghetto. To see that this is so, you need only remember how impossible most Christian groups find it to establish a relationship with people from the masses of those who have no belief.

Since so many people have given up all Christian belief, Christians today need to force themselves to approach their neighbours and get to know them where they are, in the world as it is. More than ever, we must be properly informed about the general social, political and economic situation. So we come to discover the world which Christ rules today, but in which humanity knows nothing of Christ's lordship. This search to get to know the world as it is involves an objective desire to learn, free from prejudice. More than anybody else, Christians need to be able to stand back from events and empty them of their emotional overtones. Otherwise they too will utter stereotyped judgements and fall into one-sided opinions.

How can we make sense out of all the information we acquire? One aid is to have a network of certain features which constitute keynotes of the world we are living in:

– the masses are in quest of unity
– world population is growing enormously
– changes are happening faster and faster
– many people are suffering from hunger
– the world is split into two blocs
– people want to 'live their own life'.

1 *While Christians are increasingly devoid of any sense of the universal, the masses of mankind are in quest of unity on a planetary scale.*

In just a few short decades, distances have come to have quite a new meaning. Thanks to rapid transport, to say nothing of what is broadcast by radio and television, the world's different races are mixing more and more. Even in the farthest corners of the bush you will find a radio linking those isolated there with the events of the entire world. The earth is becoming a single human reality, with a single set of behaviour patterns. Consider the enormous success of Western clothes, not even particularly attractive, in countries which hitherto have known only their own wide gandouras or loin-cloths.

All over the world, humanity is discovering its oneness. And this is happening as rapidly as everything else happens nowadays. Certainly this must be disconcerting for people still living at the pace of years gone by. Sociologically speaking, Christians form a social group of ancient origin. So, far too often, they find it impossible to grasp that in this lightning-quick development of the world there is such a tendency for the ways and means of life to unify. They lag far behind. Then the Church is ignored and, when it does come into the public eye, it is frequently judged harshly. It is seen as an out-dated social structure, incapable of keeping up with the times.

Certain Christians find this slowness hard to accept. They opt for radical ways and in some cases break all ties with the rest of those who, like them, bear the name of Christ. Their patience has been tried too far.

How true it is that the world of the poor is a goad digging deep into our flesh! Here we are, Christians, splintered into denominations; we are even incapable of showing one another the love of Christ! And right before our eyes, the masses without God are intent on finding new ways of really living together as brothers and sisters, fully open to all that is human.

Among non-believers working in this way for the brotherhood of all, you often find a lucidity, a capacity for self-criticism, and a kindness far removed from what you see in so many Christian circles. There everybody seems intent on watching all that the others are doing, only interested in defending a limited number of narrow objectives.

This disturbing fact has led Christians to run away from the Church and to try and live without it, in the midst of a world not at all interested in what we stand for. The simple fact that such separations occur is a judgement weighing heavily on us all. And consider the true gravity of the cleft between the world and Christianity as it now is: the Gospel, that leaven of communion, is no longer part of the dough.

We must understand the underlying causes of this quest of the masses today. And then we must learn to accept the present situation from the very bottom of our hearts, because by it Christians are being indirectly called to realise one essential aspect of their vocation: the catholicity, the universality of the Church. Finally, it is up to us to find a mode of Christian presence valuable for all time, by situating our life in the midst of the tension 'Church and world'. This is possible for those who refuse to condemn out of hand the often anarchic impulses of the contemporary world; for those prepared to get their hands dirty, never looking for their own private salvation without that of society at large. Different people live out this tension in different ways. Some struggle in a life lived at the heart of the masses. Others strive to know better and to explain to others the world of which Christ is Lord. Others enter upon the way of prayer, since contemplation too can be a means of being authentically present in the world.

2 *World population is expanding at an unprecedented rate.*

When the twentieth century began, one half of the total population of the world was Christian. By the year 2000, only one person in six or so will perhaps be a Christian. Some statistics: in 1900, after the great missionary expansion of the last century, out of a total world population of one and a half billion, there were some 800 million Christians, or in other words one Christian for every two human beings. At the moment it can be said that one person in four is a Christian, since the world contains some 3·8 billion people and the total number of Christians is more or less at a standstill. Meanwhile, the population as a whole is continuing its dramatic growth.

We find a particular concentration of this growth in the Far East, in regions where Christians are nothing but a tiny minority. The Church is confronted with an entirely new situation. Most of the countries where Christians are numerous have relatively stable population growth. It is those peoples whose population is exploding who are frequently full of resentment and violence against everything that comes from the Northern hemisphere, the Church included.

How are Christians going to react to this constant growth in world population?

It is clear that we need to employ scientific methods if

we want to grasp the real significance of the population increase at any given point on the globe. Statistics, charts and many other aids are available to help us understand better the sociological developments now in progress. The Church too publishes informative statistics about itself.

But simply understanding facts at this level can make hypocrites of us. We become experts on the world situation, and on the various solutions which people ought to be adopting. Then we stop half way. Uncovering the true scale of the dramatic questions confronting us today must serve to stimulate us to become men and women who are called to put concrete solutions into practice.

Here, too, informed prayer is an excellent method open to everyone. Faithfully committing to the Lord of the Church the situations of given nations or peoples, we remain present and attentive to the drama of life today. Intercession thus implies being open to all that concerns the masses of humanity.

To pray for all who live without God in the world is already a preparation of the ground for mission. But in the last resort, our response will only be completely adequate if the Christians living at the heart of the expanding peoples are seeking a truly missionary style of presence.

This is where we realise that whenever we encounter those who refuse us or who know nothing of us, we present Christians as a divided people, at loggerheads with one another. How could mankind ever come to believe that Christ is God's Son, when they do not see Christians united in their faith or their witness? The population explosion may turn out to be a powerful factor spurring Christians on towards visible unity.

It must be stressed that to use the word 'missionary' does not necessarily imply evangelising in the traditional sense of the term. Often in the past the Gospel was imposed with the help of the colonising powers; the compromises which this involved now have to be cleared up. Today we have to find ways of rehabilitating the white Christian, from the Northern hemisphere and therefore discredited; this may lead some people to be witnesses to the Gospel simply by their discreet presence. We know that we are bearers of Christ, his ambassadors. This we can be humbly, living hidden at the heart of the masses. In so doing we show that the Gospel is really unselfish.

3 *Changes are taking place faster and faster.*

Only a few facts are necessary to make us realise how rapid the acceleration has been.

In agriculture, from the end of the Roman empire until the late nineteenth century, methods of harvesting in Europe remained unchanged. In the last fifty years the scythe has been replaced by combine harvesters. In communications the evolution is even more staggering. Air travel has united humanity. Previously our geographical frontiers had always been hard and fast boundaries.

Things have reached such a pitch in North America that history books need to be published in revised form every year. Far-reaching changes no longer take decades, but are the work of a few weeks or months. So, for example, the things which we in Europe knew about the situation of blacks in the big cities of the United States a few years ago have nothing to do with the situation as it is now. Almost certainly it would be possible to make the same kind of discovery in vast regions of the USSR.

It used to take centuries for a city with all its organisation and structures to emerge; now new cities spring up in a couple of years where before there was nothing. Cities become centres to which all the people drift who have no reason for staying in underprivileged rural areas. But the cities are not able to absorb these sudden influxes of population, and so they spawn slums. Every city of bright lights has cities of distress trailing in its wake.

The atomic era has scarcely begun. What further huge transformations are lying in wait for the people of every continent? The changes have acquired an impetus that carries them faster and faster. We have reached a point in the twentieth century where we cannot imagine where these processes which the nineteenth century set in motion are going to lead us, even in the very short run.

4 *More and more people in the world are starving.*

The nations with enough have more than ever, while those with almost nothing have less than they had before. Famine and population explosion coincide. Today this is explained in part by a physiological phenomenon. The absence of certain foodstuffs stimulates an increase in hormones necessary for procreation, so that population growth is more rapid in the under-developed lands. This in turn leads to a growing lack of alimentary resources.

The Christian nations are rich in so many ways. How are we going to change the existing state of affairs so as to share our bread with those who are starving? Can we pray for people who are destitute without doing something about our excess wealth? The Gospel challenges us to respond: are we going to share our food with those who are hungry? The Christians of the twentieth century will be judged in large part by future generations on the solution which they find, or stimulate others to find, to this problem.

5 *Today's world is divided between two superpowers which seem to stand for two rival ideologies.*

In what manner are we going to be present in the tension existing between East and West? Christians are not entitled to opt out of the world's tensions, but neither are they entitled to surrender to the impassioned attitudes which those tensions provoke. More than ever they are called to be people of peace. How else can they be 'in the world but not of the world'? When our hearts are at peace before God, we will help others to forget their fear, the source of hatred and wars.

As Christians, we must admit how enticing the world can be, and recognise the enormous secularising power it can have. In the West, this secularising power consists first and foremost in all kinds of material aids by which life is made easier. So great is our ease, that it drugs us until we lose all concern for our neighbour. When such aids no longer serve a precise purpose, it is better to get rid of them. In the countries of the Eastern bloc, a Christian is equally exposed to secularising influences. The cult of the masses and the sense of their unity, as well as the overriding concern to redistribute wealth, can create a mirage that it would be easy to chase, to the detriment of what is essential in the Gospel.

If the tension between East and West continues, serious attempts will be made to persuade us that as Christians we ought to align ourselves with one or the other of the opposing systems. Then there will be times when our only course is to refuse, for motives of conscience, to be drafted into any system or party. To live at the heart of these tensions, never has it been more vital for Christians to maintain at all costs one basic condition: the freedom of the Gospel, which necessarily supposes that individuals remain free to live the Gospel. That freedom must never be confused with some kind of human liberalism. In the face of present events, we must learn not to let purely emotional reactions cloud our judgements. As we strive to attain this degree of self-control we become people of God, and that means people of peace.

6   *Those now growing up are determined to 'really live their lives'.*

In claiming the right to live as they think best, the younger generations show their determination to fulfil their human possibilities. History and all that the past offers are viewed with suspicion; what counts is direct, here-and-now experience, living fully in the present rather than becoming a part of any pattern or system. Perhaps this sense of urgency springs from an awareness of living on borrowed time, with the past poised on the verge of destruction and perhaps a whole civilisation with it.

'Self-fulfilment' is often given as the ultimate goal, and that includes the emancipation of the senses. This results in a sexualisation of our whole way of life, which is at once exploited in ways that can be seen everywhere. In America, Europe or elsewhere, on the streets, in advertisements, in films, in much of the press, everything invites people to let themselves go. There have never been so many songs proclaiming the joys of physical love, and you can hear the same song on radios from Paris via Tokyo to New York. Sometimes this frantic urge to live is justified by half-digested theories gleaned from psychology or psychoanalysis.

Christians must see clearly where their responsibilities lie in this situation, remembering that the Gospel too professes a form of existentialism, a call to live to the full each present day, given by God. Joy disappears for the Christian anxious about the future. There is a kind of folly in the Gospel that runs counter to the human longing for security.

Nothing would be easier than to adopt a puritanical attitude towards present-day culture, trying to stir up a sense of guilt among Christians with regard to the life of the senses. Immature minds in the past have sometimes been influenced by such methods. Today the results may well be very different. Any hardening, any categorical judgements on our part will only serve to alienate the younger generations from us for good. The only way forward is for us to remain fully human. This we are when we are capable of helping others find moral controls which they are prepared to apply to themselves, without any outside pressures.

Our way of being present to the world will be more persuasive than anything we say. Christians who live authentically the signs of contradiction which the world finds in the life-long faithfulness of Christian marriage, or in the calling of Christ to a life of celibacy, can be sure that the grain of wheat thrown into the ground will keep on growing, by night and by day.

LIFE IN OURSELVES

Life in Ourselves

Anyone who sets out to write about the Christian's inner life must begin by recalling that all spiritual disciplines are relative methods. It is always easier to write about them than to live them.

Our inner life must be a driving force for our entire being – body, soul and mind. Watchfulness should never be limited only to our thoughts or to our body. The physical and the psychical are so closely related and interdependent that any disorder in one brings about a disorder in the other.

Spirit and body are one. To keep them open and available for God to act is the basis of our whole inner combat. The aim is to maintain the creature in a constant communion with his Creator, with one purpose in view: the lordship of Christ Jesus over our entire being.

INNER LIFE AND COMBAT FOR CHRIST

Is it correct to think of our inner combat for Christ in terms of subduing the material to the spiritual, accelerating the death of the body with all its senses? Is living a question of 'applying ourselves to die', as Plato put it?

No such dualism of 'spirit versus matter' exists in the Gospel. On the contrary, God has become flesh; he put on a human body and dwelt among us.

The combat of life is not a struggle where the human spirit strives to conquer the body and subdue it; it is the struggle of the Spirit of God eager to dispose freely of all our human capacities in order to be able to act in them.

Christian discipline is not based on a morality of things to be given up. Self-discipline is not an end in itself; it is a way for us to respond to grace. That is not to say that the recommendation to cut off our hand if it causes us to fall does not suggest that, if every other means of healing has been tried in vain, in certain cases self-discipline may involve quite drastic measures. But no doctor will amputate unless everything else has been tried and has failed.

We respond to God's grace by submitting ourselves to his Spirit. We do not have to worry about what we ought to be giving up. Self-mastery is a big enough programme in itself. Instead of doing more than God asks of us, it is better to carry out in all simplicity what is necessary in our present circumstances. Unconsciously, our heart may prefer to follow ideal, heroic demands rather than those corresponding to our daily realities. We are simply invited to follow patiently in the way God traces; instead, we refuse the gifts offered and indulge in vain introspection, paying more attention to our sinfulness than to God's incomprehensible forgiving, trying to find private cures for our secret evil; and all the time God is offering us remedies by the means of grace available in his Church.

In our search for greater self-mastery, it is important not to attach too much importance to details, be they steps forward or backward, but rather to keep our eyes fixed on the goal, Christ Jesus himself. Otherwise we begin to mistake the means for the end, and find ourselves thinking more about ourselves than about God. We remain in sorrow over our faults instead of experiencing a constant wonderment at God's forgiveness.

Is there no risk that our inner combat will lead us into false attitudes such as formalism or perfectionism? These are dangers which need to be recognised for what they are, but that does not mean coming to a standstill and being rooted to the spot for fear of them. Living a Christian life is like walking along the brow of a steep ridge. God alone can maintain the firm footing of those who accept the Christian risk, which is to run towards Christ.

Formalism and habit? They are ever there, waiting for us to fall into them whenever our inner combat has ceased to be stimulated by the love of Christ and our neighbour. It is good to decide to pray regularly at certain hours, but for love of the Lord, not because of some law. There will certainly be days when this regularity will be burdensome. We have a nature which is in revolt against its Lord. But it is only when we let our love for Christ dry up completely that we are in danger of experiencing our former resolutions to pray or meditate regularly as a new legalism.

Here is something to remember: apply yourself to faithfulness more in times of spiritual dryness than in those periods when faith breaks spontaneously into prayer and recollection. Bear in mind all that you received in times past, the hours rich with God's presence. The only remedy for formalism and habit lies in remaining faithful to the resolution we once made, and in always attempting to carry it out with fervour and in a spirit of adoration.

'Those who have accomplished most turn out to be people who have succeeded in ordering their lives calmly and firmly, especially if they have managed to combine this firmness with a liveliness and warmth which do not always go hand in hand with an orderly, methodical spirit; combined, they make a person capable of the most astonishing things.' (A. Monod)

For our inner life, we need a few simple words to serve as basic guidelines. Otherwise we run the risk of forgetting even our very finest resolves. It is also important to condense vital elements of the Gospel into a few sentences easy to remember.

These few words must express the mind of Christ in a vocabulary suited to our mentality and having the added advantage of being very much our own. By them, the Word of God can be applied to our own particular case.

This summary – thought about deeply, worked out slowly, emerging as the fruit of a whole process of growth and often shaped through hard struggles – once discovered, must be followed. From it flows so much strength for our inner living: we no longer feel obliged to try and do everything at once; we can resolutely devote ourselves to what we undertake. It confers unity to our inner self, leading us as it does in directions which will remain constant for the whole of our lifetime.

Needless to say, it is not the number of these basic guidelines which is important. What matters is to be able to follow, in each present moment, certain brief indications short enough to keep echoing in our minds, indications we have decided to make the basis of our whole life, and to which we always return after moments of forgetfulness. If they come to be forgotten, we need to recall them vigorously as soon as we notice. They will become easy if we live them boldly. If we are really patient, not trying to pick the fruits before they are ripe but prepared to take time, we shall see the day dawn when things which once took a lot of effort on our part seem to have become quite easy. Our inner self will have been moulded without our having realised it.

The aim is to create a central unity for us to persevere in, on the basis of which we can accept the need to keep starting all over again. Christian living is an endless beginning, as we return in grace day by day, or even hour by hour, to him who forgives after every lapse and so makes all things new.

When days of fatigue come, it is essential to carry on with this inner combat, perhaps groaning as we live it without joy or love. If it should become impossible for us to continue at all, then all that remains is to abandon ourselves to Christ. When the inner flame seems dead we can still wait in silence, remembering that 'from the hardened ground a rose has sprung'.

INNER LIFE AND CONTEMPLATION

In our inner life, a communion grows up between us Christians and Christ, a personal relationship, renewed by prayer and meditation, by receiving the Body and Blood of Christ. Through it we come to grasp in contemplation something of God's presence.

Our Western ways of thinking can easily put up resistances to such forms of communication. A set, juridical mentality was a feature of ancient Rome, and it was handed down to all of Western Christianity. It left us ill-prepared for contemplation, the culmination of the inner life. In contrast, Eastern Christianity is still today rich in lives centred on just this reality. When the mind is less concerned with defining how we know God and what we know of him, there is more room available in which to adore him.

When Western Christians are confronted by a part of the Gospel their intelligence cannot make much of, they are inclined to feel dissatisfied. Our faith is always being squeezed into rational categories, and that is a sure way of making the salt lose all its taste. We become so upset at not being able to understand something that the source intended to refresh our inner life eventually runs dry on us.

Sometimes contemplation is defined in a very negative fashion, being seen as the opposite of action. It would then be a luxury reserved for those Christians who are not willing to live out their beliefs in society. The facts contradict this whole approach. There are Christians who have been very involved in the concerns of their time, veritable whirlwinds of activity, and have at the same time experienced contemplation in all its fullness. Saint Teresa of Avila was buying houses, doing business and writing books at the same time as she was living united with God in the depths of her heart. It is clear why she has remained one of the classic examples of the true contemplative.

So if we stop reacting negatively, what are we to understand by contemplation? Nothing other than that state of being in which we are totally seized by the reality of the love of God. When our mind grasps a truth of the natural order, there may be a sense in which that takes hold of us, but only partially. But our whole being, including our affections, can be caught up by that supernatural truth which is the love of God. It can be said that love is the touchstone in all this: as we enter upon the love of God, contemplation refers us back to the love of our neighbour. John is the contemplative apostle and he reminds himself of the hypocrisy of all those who say that they love God, but at the same time hate their fellows.

Contemplation strengthens our love for God. And if it is authentic, the fact of loving Christ with every scrap of our being is bound to show itself in the way we act. The love we show towards others is always the sign that our contemplation is real.

Before my eyes I have two men, both of whom have received the same vocation.

One of them is at a complete standstill; the other is running. He has learned how to 'throw away all the unnecessary burdens . . . and run . . . fixing our eyes on Jesus'. Both of them are equally intent on fulfilling their task.

One is in constant pain. He has grown over-sensitive to how others react. He is incapable of renewing in every new encounter that inner sense of mercy which enables us to accept others as they are. The other receives the same kind of wounds yet remains almost invariably joyful. One would prefer to die rather than live in God; the other is concerned solely with a charity that every contact with others reinvigorates.

This is disturbing to see. In one, mercy and even the simplest sense of pardon have died away, and so life in contact with other people has become unbearable. Whereas the other, who lives by Christ's presence, finds himself helped along by his difficulties in dealing with others, and not brought to a halt by them.

One intense conviction: any communication with God leads us towards our neighbour. The sign which proves the authenticity of our inner life – of our relationship with Jesus Christ – is how attentive we are to others. If our neighbours vanish from our dialogue with Christ, then our love for God has more to do with some mythical deity completely detached from human concerns than with the Christ of the Gospel. In those without God, love devours the soul; in Christians the soul suffocates if love for God precludes love for others.

28

Contemplation allows us to grasp a part of God's truth in love. It is given to those whose hearts are simple. A person's heart can only hold a small number of basic truths. Once they have been grasped, they have still to be worked out. The path of our Christian living passes through light and shadow, from forgetfulness of the treasure received to the sudden realisation of its full value.

Happy the simple, those possessing a spirit of simplicity, for the Kingdom is theirs. Religious knowledge, or theology and much studying, give no extra privileges in our contemplation of the 'divine mystery'. More often than not they only serve to divert our attention from it. In this we can discover something of God's justice at work, granting to the small and meek of this world a revelation of his presence. The only way is to 'keep all these things and ponder them in one's heart', to live the presence of God we have discovered face to face.

When the Lord cares for somebody in this way, it is not conspicuous. When blessings are too visible, there is reason to suspect that the self remains central at a time in which God is all. That would be a sign that our contemplation was illusory. People who seek God by prayer and fasting are told, are they not, to anoint their heads with perfume, so that nothing betrays to others their secret desire?

Contemplation remains a way open to every Christian. True, few people experience prayer as a thirst. This explains the weariness of so many convinced Christians faced with the difficulties of dialogue with God. There are people who see months, or even years, go by without being able to find any way of encountering God in prayer. Should we then talk of spiritual dryness, of the dark night of the soul? Not at all. It may rather be that in just this way we are being called towards contemplative prayer. A silence gradually settles in us, in which all the world's values become relative; only one thing becomes necessary. A difficulty about how to express ourselves as we pray may be a call to live in communion with Christ, but a communion stripped of every exterior element.

So contemplation is worshipping. Prayer leads us into

a dialogue; in it we conceptualise situations as we bring them into the field of our awareness in order to offer them to God. And meditation implies a search that may be strenuous. But in contemplation, our eyes are fixed on a single truth to which we adhere with every fibre of our being.

Since it involves the totality of our being, the contemplation of the God of Jesus Christ can never lead to quietism. On the contrary, it bears us along into risks and action, with no possibility of remaining lukewarm. It hurls us straight into the race. Any runner needs to have at least an inkling of what lies ahead. And when our race is inspired by the vision of Christ, we know where we are heading. To run properly two things are important: 'forget what lies behind', progress or setbacks . . . 'fix your eyes attentively on the Guide of your faith'.

It is the fact of looking towards the invisible Christ that determines the transformation of our whole being. These changes may be imperceptible, and they are better so; it is enough to know that by night and by day the seed takes root and grows, without our knowing how.

Running, then, being actively involved. And for the race fixing our eyes on the God of the prophets and of Christ, until the day comes when Christ himself fixes his eyes on us. Only those who have met him are capable of merciful love which overflows towards their neighbour. Happy the humble whose hearts are pure: they see God!

LIFE IN THE WORLD

Life in the World

We have already looked at a number of major features of the world today, each time suggesting ways in which our Christian life can play its full role at the heart of the human situation in this present age. Now, there are a number of additional points which ought to be made.

SIMPLIFY THE WAY WE LIVE

As far as our material life is concerned, it is important to try to review calmly but constantly the equipment of our life and work. The aim should be to rid ourselves quietly of all that is no longer relevant or necessary, that sooner or later is likely to become a hindrance. Reserves – be they furniture, books, papers, archives or clothes – can gradually wrap us round with a cloak of steel, until we are completely paralysed and unable to move in any new direction.

In the field of knowledge, this attempt to simplify and to remain simple encourages us to accept our limits. We are not asked to try to become encyclopedias: the strain would be too great for us. We are called to build in ways possible for us as the limited human beings we are. Let genius be genius. Remember all the minds which today are sick simply because people have worn themselves out trying to acquire too high a level of knowledge. It is wiser to remember what certain scholars have said: two hours of intelligent, creative effort day after day are enough to produce a very solid piece of intellectual work.

This also applies to the Gospel. We have to admit frankly that we are never going to be able to understand fully all that the Scriptures say. We find ourselves having to put into practice just the very small part we have assimilated, because it has struck a deep chord within us. That will be enough for our inner self to grow and mature, and it will lead, in time, to the unification of our personality.

UNDERSTAND EVERYONE AS THEY ARE

We have to look for a Christian form of involvement within the human society around us; we have to find, in our work and in the places where we work, a means of reflecting the presence of Christ – that may not mean talking about him. It obliges us to take people as they are, piercing below the surface so as to understand them from within, from the heart. From that moment on there can no longer be any question of judging and condemning others, but only of loving them with a love which understands everything. The worldly-wise know little of what the Gospel says, but they do know that we stand for brotherly love. Sometimes they expect us to practice to such an extent the Gospel we profess that we are taken aback, but we must be attentive to their attitude and try to live up to it. Young people especially demand authenticity, and they cannot stand tricky, pharisaical Christians with their artificial ways of avoiding the issue. Hence the need for our lives as Christians to have firm roots in the real-life situations of the world today.

WEAK WITH THE WEAK OF THE WORLD

The public mind is very much inclined to confuse being Christian with being influential and powerful. Today this obliges us to reestablish clearly what being Christian does involve, by refusing strenuously every kind of collusion between the spiritual and the temporal. Since the Lord, by his coming, 'lifted up the humble and set down the mighty', how can we still go looking for help from the powerful? The younger generation, with their horror of power being wielded in any way by the Christian community, calls us to heel often enough on this issue. Their brutal judgements in these matters may at times be unjust, but nevertheless they can give us a salutary jolt.

Being human, we have a positive need to assert ourselves, and that often degenerates into a lust for power and strength. Just where these inner drives come from is a complex question and one hard to analyse. But problems of a personal nature in no case justify human power being wielded within the framework of the Church.

Does this mean that we ought to be working out a Christian spirituality of failure and weakness, or even of utter abasement? Such extremes of faith should be left to great saints. What we need is rather to hold to a spirituality of limited-ness, with its basis in the reminder that 'it is when we are weak that we are strong' in God. Realising that our possibilities are limited, and recognising the thorns in our flesh, we always remember that in Christ we are victorious, so as to live in the joy of the Kingdom.

This will bring us closer to the weak of this world. The Kingdom is theirs. Happy the poor.

LIFE IN THE CHURCH

Life in the Church

The coming generations will have less and less patience with the contradiction of Christians split up into different denominations, with all the energy lost defending opposing viewpoints, at a time when the population explosion is rapidly increasing the number of people with no knowledge of God. They will find it intolerable that the best of Christians' time and energy is going to waste in justifying their respective positions.

Every ecclesiastical body bears within itself the seeds of self-perpetuation and self-justification, and today this fact has brought us to a standstill. At first sight the sickness seems to be without cure. So often you find men and women who began to live as newly-converted believers full of a burning love for Christ and for others, only to end up completely fossilised in their particular Church group and adopting attitudes of intransigence and self-satisfaction incompatible with the first outburst of faith. The poison of division is a subtle one, not felt by those it affects. Such people can set out wholeheartedly to live a Christian life, and yet only ten or twenty years later they seem to have lost every spark of fire or love, concerned chiefly with safeguarding a so-called spiritual heritage. This defensiveness is rooted in those human mechanisms that underlie separatism of whatever form.

Under the circumstances how can we keep alive our hope in the universality of the Church's mission, a matter of life and death for the Gospel today as never before?

39

The Gospel summons us to reach out towards every human being; in each one of us it sets a leaven of universality. But our divisions, by imprisoning us in Christian ghettos, have robbed us of all strength to face up to these demands.

This explains why today, once and for all recognising the scandal of our separations, we are striving for visible unity, the expression of an authentic communion. That alone can liberate the energies necessary for an outward-looking mission, reaching out to all those living in the world today. What Christians are being called to live with those not sharing their beliefs, on a worldwide scale, is sure to profit from this search for unity. From the very beginning, the Church has been called to fulfil a universal mission, because of its conviction that every person should be given the possibility of following in the footsteps of Jesus. Unity and mission cannot be dissociated.

We can take as our inspiration the prayer of Christ which serves as the basis for all our work towards outward-looking unity: 'May they be one, as we are one . . . so that the world may believe that you have sent me.'

Just before he died, Christ sensed all the drama of our divisions. So before leaving us he prayed more ardently than ever: let them be one. Those words are a call to unity addressed to the Christians of every period in history. If those who confess his name fight among themselves, if there is no real communion uniting them all, the world will never be able to believe that Christians see themselves as children of the same loving Father. Hypocrisy, which Christ so abhorred among the Pharisees, will once again appear in the world, this time thanks to Christians themselves.

'Christ cannot be divided.' The Body of Christ is one. All who bear the name of Christian have to be careful that their conflicts never become a stumbling-block for those unable to believe. Do we realise just how entitled the world is to laugh at us? Here we are, eagerly confessing a God of love, yet full of contempt for others who bear Christ's name just as we do. It is not surprising that our witness remains sterile before the un-Christian masses throughout the world.

Once a certain number of people become conscious of the existence of the non-Christian masses, with their hostility towards those who look to Christ, and realise how urgent our unity is, the effect will be to instil a basic sense of catholicity. A breath of fresh air will blow through the various denominations, and one question will come increasingly to the fore: what does it mean to belong to the Church as the Body of Christ? Increasingly generous and open, and truly caring for all, those who believe will come to recognise what universal values are implicit in the Church's unity. It is not merely a question of liking the few people who confess Jesus Christ in the way I do, and who pray in my fashion. After all, if I only love those who love me, what is so extraordinary about that? Surely agnostics do as much, if not more.

It is a question of seeing that if the household is divided within itself, then it is likely to collapse: on the day he returns, will the Son of Man still find faith on earth? Do we realise fully the drama playing itself out in and against the Church? If we persist in facing the world with our divisions, what will become of our message? Mankind in general sees more lucidly than we do the lack of consistency between what we say and how we live.

True, some Christians affirm that the unity of the Church already exists in Christ, invisibly. But what kind of unity is that, spiritual but incapable of showing itself in reality? After all, how can we expect those whom the Gospel terms 'the world', those without faith, to see things with the eyes of faith? The world believes what it can see, and at the moment it sees a splintered Christianity. Nothing other than a visible relationship of communion uniting us all can prove to the world that we are children of one Father, faithful to the one Christ.

This means that if we seek visible communion between Christians, it is purely in obedience to the will of Christ expressed in his last prayer: let them be one, so that the world can believe. Only in this spirit does it become possible to investigate what the conditions for real

ecumenism are, a search for communion involving a purification on all sides, in a common love for Jesus Christ.

Before we tackle the ways towards unity, it is important to set aside a number of false directions.

'*Confusionism*'. There are Christians not willing to recognise the reasons for our divisions at all. They feel that
for unity to be achieved, it is enough to confess the name
of Jesus, and insist that the divisions are only a matter of
psychology, history or mere words. That is over-sim-
plifying matters. Real ecumenism requires clear-sight-
edness and courage. Nothing is helped if we refuse to
recognise the real causes of division by not distinguishing
the points of non-agreement.

Of course, some people are tempted to reject every step
towards Christian unity by labelling it 'confusionism'
from the very start. This cuts away the ground from
under our feet at every turn.

The term 'confusionism' can only be applied when the
goal is not visible, outward unity, but mere compromises
in spite of which the unity remains invisible.

Common-sense pragmatism. Here all disagreements are
attributed to the diabolical role played by theologians.
No effort is made to understand their work, and unity is
looked for purely in terms of practical living. This way of
thinking sees social, humanitarian programmes as the
means of uniting Christians beyond their different labels,
as offering in themselves the solution to all the difficulties theologians have created. In fact, this is a totally
inadequate conception of what unity involves. That is not
to say that it is not wonderful when Christians collabor-
ate in a common service of love: nothing can better help
to prepare the ground for a total communion in the faith
itself.

Another suggestion sometimes heard is that we join in
a common fight against materialistic values, a kind of
anti-atheist crusade. The idea of Christians joining forces

to fight against other human beings would certainly be hard to reconcile with love for our neighbours! Besides, the only witness which will ever have any impact on the world is precisely our communion as Christians in peace.

Federation. It is important to set aside any idea of unity as a simple federation of various Church bodies. When ordinary social groups are involved, perhaps an administrative federation can be a good way of working hand in hand. But that has nothing to do with the deep communion characteristic of the mystical Body of Christ Jesus.

Unity in the Kingdom. Sometimes unity is said to be impossible, that it can only exist invisibly between many smaller groupings of Christians. Then, at the end of time, with the return of Christ, it will become manifest. Of course, the return of Christ will be the moment when all are gathered in oneness around the one great Shepherd of the flock. But what about the scandal of today's obvious, visible divisions between those confessing faith in a common Lord? We cannot say absolutely that unity is bound to come about at a given moment of history. It will be given in the ways and at the time willed by God. But ecumenism is a movement provoked by the Holy Spirit in order to bring together all Christians visibly and clearly within the existing order of time and space.

Unity now! We are impatient. The Lord knows the need for patience. There are maturing processes which take time. It would be wrong to try to force reunifications when these are not an organically matured expression of communion. Such reunifications would be the collective form of individual proselytising. Is that obedience to God's patience?

There are two inner attitudes incompatible with ecumenism:

Sectarianism. It is found in every field of human thought. The temptation is a subtle one: taking delight in one's own self as expressed in one's particular way of thinking, and falling prey to the resulting conviction of one's own superiority. It is important to recognise that we all can fall into this trap, especially if we have a theological vocation.

Defending the whole truth. When the avowed aim is to transmit the full spiritual heritage of the Christian Church to the coming generations, and to defend the integrity of our belief, then who would dare to say that this is not an attitude worthy of a follower of Christ?

But just as sectarianism, under the pretext of defending the truth, hardens into a fierce opposition towards others, so integral conservatism also becomes rigid, brutal, categorical. The scene turns into a battlefield – there is no question of truthfulness in love – where a war is constantly being waged to defend what is seen as an inviolable spiritual heritage. In every denomination this attitude can be found. The ecumenical movement, by promoting dialogue between the members of different Churches, has helped create a new climate. Although the Orthodox Church, for example, claims to possess the whole truth, it has still been ready to take part in this movement, and in so doing it has allowed many Protestants to discover truths about the Church which they had not encountered previously.

Now let us look at the basic attitudes inspiring Christians in their search for visible unity.

Dialogue. Instead of those long-drawn-out monologues in which we only listen to the sound of our own voices, how can we learn to listen to others so as to understand their thoughts and positions from within? Dialogue is a process of not simply clinging to my own way of seeing, and employing only the forms and categories of systems in which I feel at home; it means replying to others in their own terms, in order to broaden the systems involved. In a true dialogue there is no room for argument and polemics; it involves the decision to see others as they wish to be seen, not distorted by the image that centuries of fruitless conflict may have transmitted to us of them. Dialogue requires mutual encounter, an 'interpenetration' by which we become familiar with theologies, philosophies, a spirituality and sometimes even a whole scale of values so different that they seem to have nothing in common with our own. And doing this solely because we must love one another in truthfulness. That means taking the time needed, finding the right tone, reducing mistrust and suspicion, showing ourselves as we really are. Dialogue is the opposite of debate and attack.

Centuries have taught us to condemn each other loftily and from a respectable distance. It is always easy to judge others brutally when our opinions can rain down on fellow Christians from the lofty heights of our own securities. But total comprehension lies in love. Comprehension does not just mean knowing by heart the viewpoints of the other party; it is the attempt to love the reasons underlying them, the processes involved, and the end-results. Loving the others' positions as they have evolved in the course of Church history. Trying to enter into their praying and their thinking, so as to know why my neighbour thinks and prays in ways which are different from mine.

Purity of intention. No afterthoughts must enter into this quest for dialogue. We are together because God has called us, not with the idea of converting the other. Anyone who sets out on the quest for unity with the premeditated intention of winning others over to his or her side betrays the whole ecumenical spirit. Purity of intention opens the way to balanced, thoughtful exchange, the forerunner of great new things in the Church of Jesus Christ. When trust is complete, we can undertake the honest exchanges which will allow our comprehension to deepen.

Prayer. If there is no prayer for unity, ecumenical work is bound to remain dry and fruitless. When confronted with all the difficulties accruing from sin and human traditions of every kind, at times when we are at the end of a road with no apparent exit ahead of us, it is praying which renews our hopefulness and love. In prayer for unity, we ask the Lord for mercy, humbling ourselves for our own wrongs and the obstacles we set in the way. We pray for all the people in the world working for unity, so as to see them become in God and by God instruments of his communion. Prayer also obliges us to see the full dimensions of the Church, by placing us within the communion of saints. And thanksgiving has its place, too, when we think of all that God, who alone is the author of our communion, has already brought about. His promises offer us a sure resting-place.

Patience. All prayer and all action must always be set under the sign of God's patience. We know that God's ways are not ours. If we are to discover them, then patience has to be a fundamental value of ecumenical dialogue. How could all our centuries-old divisions simply vanish overnight? That would suppose changes far beyond anything that, humanly speaking, we can imagine. God is at work; we are his workers. We are called to persevere in work and prayer, always and faithfully.

Poverty before God. Any who have been called to work for communion, be they lay people or theologians, must always pay special attention to the humblest, simplest members of the People of God. One poor woman, with a single, awkward gesture, can express such a degree of fervour that we are obliged to become less rigorous in our categories and recall that Christian truth is expressed throughout the whole People of God. Each person receives his or her own share, the charism by means of which they can contribute to the mind of the Church. But all must be attentive to the faith which completes their own, because all together compose that perfect harmony of the great choir of the communion of saints.

Looking attentively towards the humblest makes us recall the prophetic vision which allowed the Virgin Mary to proclaim that by Christ's coming the weak and poor are lifted up, the strong and impressive set down . . . and are not those of us who occupy positions of responsibility within the Church often among the strong of this world?

LIFE AT THE CROSSROADS
OF CHURCH AND WORLD

Life at the Crossroads of Church and World

When we see how urgent and how vast is the question of our Christian presence both at the heart of the life of the one, universal Church and in the midst of present day human living, it may seem pretentious to talk here about the very modest answers emerging from Taizé. We see clearly the lack of proportion between our searching, as the fragile persons we are, and the horizons which stretch out before us, horizons so vast that we are troubled at the very sight of them. It is important to remain modest here.

But the Word has become flesh. And as witnesses to the Word we must respond, in all our human weakness, with as much lucidity and love as we can muster, to the ways in which it challenges us. For this reason our common service of Jesus Christ plays on two dominant keynotes: the quest for Christian unity, and the determination to be present at a certain number of contemporary focal-points. The whole balance of our vocation as a community lies in the tension between these two poles.

It is certain that working out such a community life in the Church and in the world means exposing ourselves to risks and difficulties. Christians are often so nervous when it comes to new experiences, so timid and so anxious to preserve conformity to the spiritual heritage handed down to them! As for the world, we run the risk of seeing it as a refuge, a place where we can breathe freely: it is often easier to find fresh air there than in a good number of aging Christian contexts.

Always the inner call to Christian unity is renewed in

us by our desire to conform wholeheartedly to the Gospel. The Gospel insists on love towards all, so it cannot give us the right to remain hostile to a particular form of Christianity. An immeasurable amount of strength flows from this determination to be consistent with our Gospel-based profession of love; it may be one of the principal means by which the divisions between Christians will one day be broken down.

Those who adopt this attitude have no intention of condemning the generations of Christians who have gone before them. They simply feel that at present they are being asked to live this unshakable resolve, finding themselves no longer able to enter into the scheme of Christian divisions. It is almost as though they have become conscientious objectors, in so far as they refuse the inconsistency represented by the continuing divisions among Christians.

We are not prepared to let ourselves be used to shore up any one particular denomination's good conscience; we intend to use the means at our disposal to try and breach the walls keeping Christians apart. Such a programme of service requires a continuity stretching over whole generations, to say nothing of a burning patience. A cenobitic community (from the Greek *koinos bios*, 'common life') can surely serve as a possible point of continuity in this sense, holding fast as waves of enthusiasm and scepticism towards Christian unity come breaking around it.

We need to be familiar with the Churches as they are today, with their treasures and their failings, and live a constant presence of prayer at the very heart of the Church's life. Otherwise, we will never be up to the difficult task involved in sending some of our brothers out to live a presence at key points of the present-day world.

Our experience has shown us that the danger of escapism (which some have claimed to see in our vocation) does not at all take the form of a withdrawal into the cosiness of Christian groupings which we have already termed the 'Christian ghetto', a world far more 'enclosed' than any convent! The real risk lies in a different direction, and is far subtler. It consists in a possible attraction to this present world. In it, we often find non-believers who are more clear-sighted and able to criticise themselves, more aware of human values, more kind and free of self-righteousness. All these qualities ought to flourish among Christians, because without them we are condemned to a slow death by suffocation. Often we have found it possible to make a fresh start out in the world, simply because we were able to breathe freely there. Now a temptation along the line of least resistance could encourage us to desert the old Christian forms altogether and live solely in the front lines of human life today.

For this reason, a risk might be involved in sending young brothers out into industrial work; they might well discover there in trade-unionism a thirst for greater justice and a determination to bring about real changes, attitudes far too often lacking among Christians, despite the longing for human justice found in the Beatitudes. As a result, before we start to build the tower we have to sit down and see just what capacities and materials we have to build with. Not all can run the risk of living dangerously, yet some people must – they have been given gifts which they owe it to themselves to use. Are Christians, who tackle life with all the power promised by the Lord of Church and cosmos, going to be the only ones who let themselves be stopped by fear of dangers, of temptation, or of the world?

The goal set before us by our vocation is the service of Jesus Christ in common. But if we say that we serve in common, that does not imply that we have to stay grouped under one roof the whole time, but that the body as a whole keeps together in spite of being spread over the world. We want our service to be daring, going to places where many Christians would be unable to go because of their responsibilities, taking our place at the forefront, in the strategic front lines of history-in-the-making.

Our vocation has taught us to find a balance in a life set at the crossroads of Church and world.

Two forms of service lay before us, contemplation and

action. They were not at all mutually exclusive, so we tried to unite the two. If our vocation had been purely a contemplative one, we would have stressed objective forms of prayer, those belonging to the Church of all the ages, without any attempt being made to go out towards modern man. But since at the same time we were driven out to live among men, our inner life has been drawn towards forms of spirituality which rather awkwardly we term 'athletic'. By that we understand a concern to remain fully human as we live our Christian lives, striving in the direction pointed out by St Paul: 'I treat my body severely, mastering it, going into training, so that after I have been a guide for others I will not be disqualified myself.'

If there were a spirituality proper to Taizé, it would simply be the desire to 'run' in St Paul's sense of the word. Running together, not each one on his own any longer, means giving up any idea of looking only for one's individual salvation, in order to strive for the salvation of all. And our race leads towards a finishing line: we can only run when we, all of us together, are focused on Christ in glory.

We draw the energy needed for such mutual training from the Church's treasury of centuries of prayer. Prayer together, wherever we are, morning, noon and evening, has been a framework for our whole common life. It is that prayer, too, which has driven us out into the world to bear witness to the joy and love of Christ.

To enable us to hold fast in God's service, we are given three great signs to live out, signs which always remind us of the absolute inherent in our vocation; it is these which make us part of the great monastic family. So it is important to stop here and go more thoroughly into each of them in turn.

CELIBACY

Celibacy

The chastity of celibacy is only possible because of Christ and the Gospel. 'To those who have left wife, children, lands . . .' it is important to remember this. If this vision is rejected, sooner or later a person is bound to fall into bitterness, failure, and perhaps even total spiritual collapse: the fullness of Christian life, certainly possible in celibacy as in marriage, will have been destroyed at its very roots.

This fact of life is so hard to grasp that nobody can be blamed for not understanding Christ's teaching on celibacy. He himself insists that 'only those to whom it is given can understand'.

We have to realise that Christ's teaching on marriage and celibacy remains as revolutionary today as on the day it was given – and to see that we need only put ourselves into the climate of the Old Covenant for a moment.

In ancient Israel marriage is seen as a natural obligation, always marked by the command to 'increase and multiply'. First and foremost, a posterity for Abraham has to be ensured; the begetting of children is stressed so that the people of Israel can be sure of surviving. But if you think how easy it is to obtain a divorce – a simple letter of divorce is sufficient – it soon becomes apparent that monogamy runs the risk of becoming polygamy by a series of monogamous relationships. In this way the original commandment is safe: 'You shall not commit adultery,' but the moral conscience of the individual is given a loophole.

Since in the eyes of religious law all must marry, it may be said that at the moment when Christ was born in Israel, no real vocation to marriage existed, since there was no free choice in the matter.

Christ came, and he established a different order of things. Henceforth in the Church, individuals have two possible vocations, both difficult, both involving self-denial, limitations and sacrifices. Truly monogamous marriage, in which there can be no question of divorce, is no more natural to the human heart than celibacy. There is no longer any need for physical descendants of Abraham. Jesus himself, truly man and fully God, accepted for himself the choice of celibacy for the sake of the Kingdom of heaven.

Marriage and celibacy are both Christian absolutes. Both, because of Christ, become signs of the coming Kingdom. Both oblige us to live dangerously in ways that can only be accepted for the sake of Christ and the Gospel.

The Reformation was preoccupied with Scriptural foundations, yet where celibacy was concerned it very often fell back into an Old Testament approach. In the sixteenth century, the main preoccupation was with certain abuses of ecclesiastical celibacy, and little attention was paid to the evangelical value of celibacy as such. At the very most, basing themselves on St Paul, people are prepared to accept the practical usefulness of not being married. Yet what constitutes the real appeal of celibacy today is much more the outrageous sign of contradiction it represents in the midst of a hardened world, which has stopped its ears and which needs clear, visible signs. In the sexualised climate of the West, a whole lifetime offered in authentic chastity for the name of Christ represents a gigantic question-mark.

Why this renunciation? Why celibacy? It springs from obedience to an evangelical order of things, which is not the same as that of nature. So celibacy finds its full value when it is incarnated in men and women who are truly beings of flesh and blood, often with souls of fire, passionate, rich in affection and human potential. With the vocation to common life, this sign of contradiction can be lived out in every kind of situation, by people present in factories, out in the fields, or in the world of scholarship.

But at this point it is worth repeating that Christian marriage and celibacy are only properly understood when they are seen as a search to obey the Lord of the Church, with the sole aim of loving him more and more. Accepted in love for Christ and for others, they will never cause any loss of openness. In the opposite case they very rapidly become the scene of regression and self-seeking: then we no longer love because of Christ and the Gospel, so that our love is no longer self-giving but aims principally at possessing and dominating. This brings even ideal couples to the point where their life together turns into a cell on the verge of collapse, because everything has been lived in function of their private, natural happiness. Or you find Christian parents who love their children only in so far as it brings them personal gratification. And unmarried people can let themselves go sliding down the same slope: over-sensitive and afraid to be open, their sensitivity turns against them, and the result is individuals whose susceptibilities are always being upset.

Unless Christ's own love takes hold of our entire being, unless we let ourselves be set on fire by his love, we shall never attain to the fullness of Christian marriage or Christian celibacy.

In all those who become part of the great monastic family, the once-and-for-all commitment to celibacy expresses their desire to become people of a single love. The monastic vocation – in the original sense of the word 'vocation to solitude' – involves those who pursue it in a form of solitude with God. So, having to love the invisible God truly without hating any of those whom we can see, all who live this vocation nourish their ability to love at the only possible source, Christ. And so, by the chastity of celibacy, they tend to become people of a single love.

A question still remains. If marriage makes such demands, how can people bind themselves for life in this way? That is more or less what the disciples wondered. As far as celibacy is concerned, we ourselves reflected about our right to bind ourselves for life: could that be a way of imprisoning the freedom of the Spirit? But then it seems as though we are simply quibbling about God's freedom in order to keep something back for ourselves, as though God were not free and powerful enough to make his calls plain. The only response we could make was to commit ourselves on the basis of Christ's promises: 'Any who leave father, mother, wife, children . . . will receive a hundredfold here and now, and eternal life in the age to come.' If we set out with Christ in a commitment, he himself sets out with us: that is a truth we have learnt by experience, and it has confirmed us in a calling that perhaps can only be fully understood by those to whom it has been given.

'Although celibacy brings greater freedom to attend to the things of God, it can only be accepted with the aim of giving ourselves more completely to our neighbour with the love of Christ himself.

'Our celibacy, means neither indifference nor a break with human affections; it calls for their transfiguration. Christ alone can convert our passions into total love of our neighbour. When selfishness is not transcended by growing generosity, when you no longer resort to confession to overcome the need for self-assertion contained in every passion, when the heart is not constantly brimming over with great love, you can no longer let Christ love in you and your celibacy becomes a burden.

'This working of Christ in you demands infinite patience.' (*The Rule of Taizé*)

The commitment to chastity is a call to live a radical transparence, in situations which may be very exposed. It is not too much to talk in terms of heroic chastity, lived out in a necessary struggle which binds us to Christ body and soul.

Transparence of heart leads us to see God: 'Happy the pure in heart, they shall see God.' We must count on this promise to see God, very soon, already in this present life. In the end it will come to be the only thing that matters. Without this longing to see Christ, there is no hope of being able to remain transparent in heart and body. Without this expectation, maintained and renewed within us by the silent contemplation of Christ our God, all limpidity is unthinkable. Unthinkable, because the definitive, once-and-for-all deprivation of all desire of the flesh, even imaginative, seems so sure to lead to a bitter revolt; unthinkable, because in every person there is such a need for total intimacy longing to find satisfaction – we must face it – on the physical level as well.

To persevere in chastity and to respond to the call to inner transparence, and thus to remain true to our deepest selves, only the desire to see Christ will ever be capable of quenching our thirst. Gradually, what is murky and unacknowledged is stirred and swept away in spite of ourselves, by the contemplation of the living Christ of the Gospels, the glorified Christ in the Church's prayer.

'Put out your eye; cut off your hand . . . if they cause you to fall.' 'Treat our bodies severely . . .' Any such battle can only be undertaken for the sake of Christ and the Gospel. It means fighting like a real athlete in the stadium, to win the prize. 'To put out an eye:' setting out to establish new patterns that allow us to triumph over psychological mechanisms that otherwise are capable, in given situations, of setting off well-known imaginative and emotional processes. And at the end of the road, the achievement of our physical life's repose with Christ in God.

It is vital to remember that no attempt at purification in order to see God can succeed without contemplation. Otherwise the ascetic discipline lashes back: it goes running after an impossible purity, until finally we come to love the discipline for its own sake, as a way of asserting ourselves.

Only when our eyes are fixed on Christ is the slow transformation possible. Gradually our natural human-love turns into a living Christ-love; we find ourselves on the far side of the difficulties. Our heart, our affections, our senses, our human nature are all present and fully alive, but with Another than ourselves transfiguring them.

61

COMMUNITY OF GOODS

Community of Goods

When everything is shared by all, the possibility of poverty can never be excluded: 'The audacity involved in putting to good use all that is available at any time, not laying up capital and not fearing possible poverty, is a source of incalculable strength. But if, like Israel, you save the bread from heaven for tomorrow, you are in danger of pointlessly overstraining the brothers whose vocation is to live in the present.' (*The Rule of Taizé.*)

In our vocation, we are always in danger of idealising poverty! But poverty was never canonised by the Gospel! For Christ, the poor are the humble of his people, or else those who refuse to use their wealth to gain power over the souls of other human beings. Christ himself lived in such a manner that he traced a way for us to follow: he finds himself in the midst of sinners and wants to gladden their hearts; well understanding their human nature, at Cana he changes the water into wine. He loves the unfortunates and reprimands hardened rich people; after all, in the last resort the land which they call theirs, and all that is in it, belongs to the Lord, does it not?

Voluntary poverty, freely accepted, can help one to live in a Christian way, and it stimulates a quality of detachment which ownership of goods certainly does not favour; but that does not mean that poverty is the ideal state for a Christian to live in. 'Poverty has no virtue in itself. The poor of the Gospel learn to live without having the next day's needs ensured, joyfully confident that everything will be provided. The spirit of poverty does not mean looking poverty-stricken, but disposing everything in creation's simple beauty. The spirit of poverty means living in the joyfulness of each present day. If for God there is the generosity of distributing all the good things of the earth, for man there is the grace of giving what he has received.' (*The Rule of Taizé.*)

Why do we tire ourselves out with so much frantic bustling around? We may not admit it, but we are all filled with shame at the very idea of being poor. Poverty is looked down on. 'What people think' has taught us that to a given education corresponds a given income. And 'education' here means a whole set of external, unreal habits, patterns of need which enslave us without our realising it. But if tonight your soul is asked of you, who will benefit from all that you have accumulated?

It is not because we profess a common life that we are delivered from worrying about our daily bread, especially when we have to earn all that we need. It becomes clear that between the words 'Each day has enough trouble of its own' and a corresponding attitude to life, there lies a whole world of difference.

Community of goods has real value only if we are ready to take risks for God, accepting with one accord whatever may arise, going if necessary to live in the poorest kind of housing and, if no resources are available, still persevering in our mission in spite of poverty.

Dare to live dangerously, setting out like Abraham who did not know where he would be led, able to abandon oneself in the confident trust that what is necessary for each day will be provided. In this way, the entire spirit of ownership is short-circuited.

Community in nothing but material goods would be very limited. It must extend to community in spiritual goods as well, the sharing of sorrows and joys.

'In the transparency of brotherly love, admit your mistakes simply, never using them as a pretext for pointing out those of others. Wherever they are, brothers practise brief and frequent sharing together.' (*The Rule of Taizé.*)

To be transparent in relationships does not mean always pouring out everything about oneself. Rather, it implies a growing limpidity of one's entire being.

Openness between brothers is not the same thing as confession. We confess to the Lord of heaven and earth, in the presence of a person who has received the ministry of reconciliation.

There were times in the Church's history when it was poverty that provided the sign of contradiction capable of touching the hearts even of people only in the early stages of evangelisation. In today's world Christians, without excluding personal poverty as a possibility, need to manifest the gift of their lives by a strong concern to see the wealth accumulated in a few privileged regions of the globe shared out among all peoples. The Church is at present challenged by a doctrine which, atheist in its premises, insists actively on the need for a redistribution of wealth.

Christians today must be either blind or paralysed if they can no longer comprehend the evangelical calling manifested by those first Christians who 'held everything in common'. They forget, or have not realised, that in the early centuries this was one of the main concerns of the Doctors of the Church, and one in which they dreaded compromise. We ought to take time to reflect upon their teaching. It will tell us all we need to know. But first, a question: the Church is always light in the darkness, so ought it not to rejoice whenever it sees the world adopting principles of community-living, turning the precepts of the Gospel into social laws? That may not necessarily imply that the world is growing more Christian. But under the influence of the Gospel, it can move towards a relative social order which the Church could always recognise as a lesser evil.

Listen to Saint Ambrose of Milan: 'The world was created in common and for all, rich and poor alike: so why do you who are rich claim to have exclusive rights of ownership over land? Nature knows no rich people; she only begets paupers ... When you give charity to the poor, it is not something you do with wealth which belongs to you. You are simply restoring to them a portion of what is theirs, because you have been usurping for yourself things that belong to the entire community and

67

were given for all to enjoy. The earth belongs to all, not just to a few rich people.'

Saint John Chrysostom is no less categorical: 'When a small number of people try to appropriate for themselves the things that belong to all, quarrels and wars break out, as though nature were indignant at the sight of the cold words "yours" and "mine", which introduce division where God has set unity . . . Those words are empty of meaning; they express no reality. You are stewards of the goods of the poor, even when you have acquired them through honest labour or by inheritance . . . The greatest harm that you suffer from being rich is that it takes you away from the happy slavery of Jesus Christ.'

Basil of Caesarea uses the same kind of language: ' "These things are mine, so surely I am entitled to keep them?" How are they yours? Where did you get them from? Did you bring them into the world? It is like someone with a ticket for one seat in the theatre wanting to stop anyone else from coming in, so as to enjoy on his own, as though by exclusive right, a show intended for the whole community. That is how the rich behave: they think that goods meant for all belong to them, just because they got hold of them before others did . . . You may call a house yours, but you have said nothing. The air and the earth, every house as well as you who do the building, all things without exception belong to the Creator . . . Community of goods is a more satisfactory norm of existence than private ownership, and it is the only natural one.'

And Chrysostom also said: 'Is it not wrong to keep for oneself something belonging to the Lord, to enjoy alone things which are for everybody? Surely "the earth is the Lord's, with all it contains". If our wealth belongs to the Lord of the world, then it belongs to all those who serve him, since everything that belongs to God is there for all to make use of.'

THE SERVANT OF COMMUNION

The Servant of Communion

In a community, the ministry of a servant of communion is a practical necessity: 'Without unity, there is no hope of bold and total service of Jesus Christ. Individualism breaks up the community and brings it to a halt.' (*The Rule of Taizé*.)

Certainly, the ideal would be to make all decisions on a unanimous basis. But idealism is not an evangelical notion. If we always had to wait for everyone to agree before we advanced, the community would very soon be at a standstill. It is vital to keep moving ahead; whoever tries to stop begins to regress. This is a fact of life.

When a common decision has to be taken, is the majority-system really the best? It is always permissible to express doubt when the Church simply borrows a procedure from human society. Is the will of the Lord clear if fifty-one per cent are in favour of something? Within a community, the use of such a method leads more or less directly to intrigues and power-struggles.

In the Church, decisions are taken in order to follow the path traced out for us by God and to lead Christians along a way of practical service. Authority in a community can only be Christ-centred. Whoever has received that responsibility is obliged, before taking practical decisions, to seek out what God intends. In this search-process all have their part to play, of course: the council, composed of all who have committed themselves for life, 'seeks all the light possible on the will of Christ for the ongoing life of the community. The first step is therefore to bring yourself into silence, to be ready to listen to your Lord. Nothing is more unfavourable to objective judgement than the ties of particular affinity, for we may incline to support a brother in the perhaps unconscious hope of obtaining his support in return at some point. Nothing is more contrary to the spirit of the council than a search which has not been purified by the sole desire to discern God's will. If there is one time when you must seek peace and pursue it, avoid disputes and the temptation to prove yourself right, it is during the council. Avoid a tone that precludes reply, the categorical "we must". Do not build up clever arguments to make yourself heard; express in a few words what you feel conforms most closely with God's plan, without imagining that you can impose it. To avoid encouraging any spirit of rivalry, the prior is responsible before his Lord for making decisions without being bound by a majority. Thus set free from human pressures, he listens to the most timid brother with the same attention he gives to a brother full of self-assurance. If he senses a lack of real agreement on an important question, he should reserve judgement and take a provisional decision, ready to review it later; standing still is disobedience for brothers advancing towards Christ.' (*The Rule of Taizé.*)

As servant of communion, the prior's charge is to lead towards Christ, to mark with the greatest possible continuity the whole community's advance towards Christ, and to preserve the community from inner divisions, since the Tempter is always at work, seeking crisis-situations and trying to divide what must remain united. Here too, we must beware of false spiritualism. If the unity is not visible, if it does not leap into sight, soon it will no longer be possible to talk of spiritual unity either.

Any mention of the charge given to someone in the Church must be accompanied by a consideration of the serious responsibilities involved: 'Making decisions is a formidable task for the prior. He should keep alert and pray so as to build up the whole body into Christ. He should look for the special gifts of each brother, so that the brother can discern them for himself. He should not consider his charge to be superior, nor must he assume it in a spirit of resignation. He should bear in mind only that it has been entrusted to him by Christ, to whom he will have to give account. He should root out all authoritarianism in himself, but never be weak, in order to maintain his brothers in God's plan. He should prevent the authoritarian from dominating and give confidence to the weak. He should arm himself with mercy and ask Christ to grant it as the grace most essential for him.' (*The Rule of Taizé.*)

By what right does a person intervene in the community? By the authority of the Word of God. The Lord of the Church lets his Word be heard by transmitting it through human lips; he gives the necessary gifts, including that of spiritual discernment. Human words have no authority in themselves. Only God gives them that.

So anyone called to announce God's Word is in an infinitely difficult situation: very often he would prefer to repel his Lord who is obliging him to speak with full authority. Will not human sinfulness affect what he says? A serious question, demanding constant watchfulness. Any who are at grips with this know that they can only exercise their ministry in a spirit of prayer; it presupposes self-denial in order to seek the sovereign Will together with all those entrusted to them. How can someone exhort and set aright, if he or she is not a living proclamation of self-forgetting? Being misunderstood, deeply disappointed, abandoned in many ways: such are the crosses which have to be borne patiently by those who exercise a ministry in the Church, and accepted as a school of humiliation.

How can we judge objectively without selflessness? Our sensitiveness and self-love are being wounded all the time; they have to be laid to rest so that God's judgement can have free range. And then, true authority is bestowed on the human word which, in the community, strives to bring together what is separated.

This ministry has nothing to do with human constraint, or the imposing of one's own will. It can never take the place of another's conscience; its role is to recall the will of Christ. A servant of communion must be on the watch against that secret form of ambition which consists in a desire to dominate souls and make them our own. Such an ambition is infinitely more perilous than that of the mighty of this world who control things and bodies. The role of a servant of communion is always to decrease, so that Christ may increase in all those entrusted to him.

AFLAME WITH CHRIST'S LOVE

Aflame with Christ's Love

If we are to keep our fire, in God's today, then the living charity of Christ must come to feed the flames with constantly renewed friendship for every human being, all our brothers and sisters.

It may seem paradoxical, but it is often easier for us to be on close terms with people unaware of God than with Christians. At the heart of human living we find so many ways of trying to offer a simple presence of Christ, of being leaven hidden in the dough, without encountering any defensive reactions. Friendship between Christians is so much more difficult! Christian societies grow old, denominational separations persist, and this makes relationships more complicated, with real friendship becoming increasingly precarious. There is the constant risk of getting bogged down in the morass of emotionally-charged reactions which have accumulated over centuries. Our capacity to act as rational human beings has been vitiated to such an extent that it becomes impossible to restore it to its true aim – the pursuit of truth in love.

It is not at all a question of betraying the truth, but we must stress the fact that there can be no truth without love. Relations between Christians today require love before anything else; once it is present, such love will lead us to refuse the all too easy and all too human attitudes by which we have learned to become judges of one another. If there is no conversion to the love of Jesus Christ, how can we ever hope to see profound changes in our denominational attitudes, which have taken shape over generations?

Part of our progress towards oneness will involve acquiring this firm hope: the Lord will surely bring us to communion, he has the power. Our task is simply not to rebel against the means he chooses to employ.

Already, many people are wondering in their heart of hearts whether they can hope for unity come what may. Yes, because that was Christ's last prayer: 'May they all be one . . . so that the world will believe.' This means that visible communion is not just a human aspiration; our faith demands it. It is not dictated by external circumstances; it is obedience to Christ.

The inner attitude corresponding to this new obedience will flow from a life lived intensely in Christ. Such a life does not foster sentimental nostalgia for unity; it is a virile force which will break down within ourselves all those forms of opposition to others which have been consuming so much of our vital energy.

Loving the Church. Loving her as Christ loved her, and accepting that she will always have to make her way across the deep-worn ruts of her children's sinfulness – their spirit of division and self-righteousness. Loving the Church, in spite of the mediocrity of some of those who bear heavy responsibilities within it. Loving the Church in its members, in the best as well as in the most compromised.

In this way the Church of Christ advances through time. It is alive to the extent that it is inspired by the love of all its faithful. It is strong when its members arm themselves, day after day, with the endless patience of faith. It is humble when its people, far from condemning with smug bitterness, are prepared to love it to the point of giving their lives, today and every day, in the attempt to renew it.

Any other road can only lead to the spirit of self-sufficiency and schism, while still not righting the wrongs condemned.

External judgements inevitably harden and imprison those who bear the brunt of them. We must admit that neither the steadfastness nor the excellent arguments of the Reformers who left their original confessions succeeded in reforming a Church whose transformation they longed for with all the hope of which they were capable. And that is not at all to underestimate the importance of the reforms they called for: they were necessary. But how can we who come after them hope for changes if the calls to renewal emanating from new forms of Christianity – so soon loaded down with layer upon layer of polemic and strife – are devoid of any love for the reality which lies hidden beneath even the most hidebound of traditions?

When our hearts are finally empty of all bitterness and open to be filled with infinite friendship towards every person we encounter, we shall find that people are able to accept our comments and our teaching. When the love of the living Christ grows within us, we find it impossible to burden others with a bad conscience. We become able to love even those who oppose us. And then a Christian can be sure of moving on firm ground, can be sure of being in God.

There is one example in history of an authentic reform: Saint Francis of Assisi. He suffered for the Church, loving it as Christ loves it. It would have been easy for him to pass harsh judgements on the institutions, the customs and the callous attitudes of some of his fellow Christians. But that is precisely what he refused to do. He chose instead to die to himself, waiting with burning patience until at last his love-filled waiting brought about renewal.

The Lord brought his People through the desert, and he has the patience to lead us still by his sovereign power. He is capable of raising up prophets from among his People.

Today, only Christ can kindle in us the fire of his love, to make us leaven in the dough. Some are called to express communion by their words, others receive the gift of fervent intercession, while others are asked to offer their lives, to make a gift of themselves which may demand a hard struggle, while the point of it all remains hidden. What matters is for each Christian, by means of these varied gifts, to become a ferment of communion in the Church.

The means at our disposal seem very slight. The yeast and the dough look so much alike that our eyes strain to see the difference. Yet invisibly the yeast contains the power to transform everything. Everything is hidden within it, and therefore the infinite becomes possible.

Yeast must always be well mingled with the dough. And each of us must be present at the heart of the Church and of the world, with that discreet presence characteristic of every life hidden with Christ in God.

What we renew is liable to harden again one day, just as the outer layer of the dough hardens with age. And so it is up to us to prepare others who will be able to put in new leaven after us. This is how Christ's Church, and those ho give it life, are renewed.

If our lives are offered in these varied ways, then although we may not know how, consequences will arise from these modest beginnings, consequences which are incalculable.

One day, says the Apostle, the gift of tongues and the gift of prophecy will disappear, knowledge will cease, but love never passes away. We may perform heroic deeds, or have faith enough to move mountains, we may give everything we own to feed the poor, and even go so far as to give our bodies to the flames; yet, without love, it will all be in vain.

We may achieve marvels, but only those will really count which result from Christ's merciful love alive within us. In the evening of life we shall be judged on love, the love we allow gradually to grow and spread into merciful kindness towards every person alive, in the Church and throughout the entire world.